FAILURE

Heartbreaks in SPORTS

Roger Sipe

Publishing Credits

Rachelle Cracchiolo, M.S.Ed., *Publisher*
Conni Medina, M.A.Ed., *Managing Editor*
Nika Fabienke, Ed.D., *Series Developer*
June Kikuchi, *Content Director*
Michelle Jovin, M.A., *Associate Editor*
Kevin Pham, *Graphic Designer*

TIME and the TIME logo are registered trademarks of TIME Inc. Used under license.

Image Credits: front cover AP Photo/Ross D. Franklin; pp.6–7 Rick Stewart/Getty Images; pp.8–9 Michael Appleton/NY Daily News Archive via Getty Images; pp.10–11 Paul Tepley Collection/Diamond Images/Getty Images; p.12 Justin Tafoya/NCAA Photos via Getty Images; pp.14–15 Lou Capozzola / Sports Illustrated/Getty Images; pp.16–17, pp.28–29 Ezra Shaw/Getty Images; pp.18–19 f11photo/Shutterstock; p.21 Elsa/Getty Images; pp.22–23 Howard Earl Simmons/NY Daily News Archive via Getty Images; pp.26–27 Nick Laham/Getty Images; pp.30–31 Francois Xavier Marit/AFP/Getty Images; pp.32–33 Steve Powell/Getty Images; pp.34–35 Jamie Francis/KRT/Newscom; pp.38–39 Josh Hedges/Zuffa LLC/Getty Images; all other images from iStock and/or Shutterstock.

Library of Congress Cataloging-in-Publication Data

Names: Sipe, Roger, author.
Title: Failure : heartbreaks in sports / Roger Sipe.
Description: Huntington Beach, CA : Teacher Created Materials, 2019. | Includes index. | Audience: Grade 7 to 8.
Identifiers: LCCN 2017055675 (print) | LCCN 2018009502 (ebook) | ISBN 9781425854928 (e-book) | ISBN 9781425850166 (pbk.)
Subjects: LCSH: Sports--Psychological aspects--Juvenile literature. | Failure (Psychology)--Juvenile literature. | Sportsmanship--Juvenile literature.
Classification: LCC GV706.4 (ebook) | LCC GV706.4 .S546 2019 (print) | DDC 796.01/9--dc23
LC record available at https://lccn.loc.gov/2017055675

Teacher Created Materials
5301 Oceanus Drive
Huntington Beach, CA 92649-1030
www.tcmpub.com
ISBN 978-1-4258-5016-6
© 2019 Teacher Created Materials, Inc.

Table of Contents

Overcoming Defeat 4

Football Frenzy 6

The Way the Ball Bounces 13

Take Your Base 20

International Incidences 26

One-on-One Losses 32

Making an Effort 40

Glossary 42

Index 44

Check It Out! 46

Try It! 47

About the Author 48

Overcoming Defeat

ABC's *Wide World of Sports* was a television program long before cable TV, ESPN, and Fox Sports. It **showcased** all sorts of athletic competitions, highlighting everything from lumberjack games to boxing to basketball. The show's introduction said it all: "Spanning the globe to bring you the constant variety of sport: the thrill of victory and the **agony** of defeat, the human drama of athletic competition."

Olympics Then and Now

The modern Olympic Games began in 1896, pitting nation against nation in various sports. The Olympics are based on competitions that began thousands of years ago. Back then, ancient Greek city-states competed in sports, such as wrestling, boxing, and racing in full armor.

Those words describe why most people watch sports—the greatest victories often go hand in hand with the greatest defeats. That is what keeps people tuning in every time their favorite teams gear up to play. But beyond the thrill of victory and the agony of defeat are great lessons to be learned about how to exhibit good sportsmanship. These life lessons are what make sports so important in our society.

Sports Can Be Good for You!

Americans love to play sports. In a 2015 Harris Poll, 73 percent of adults said they participated in some form of athletic activity when they were younger. Those adults tended to have more money and higher education levels, perhaps because of what they learned while playing.

Football Frenzy

American football is many people's favorite sport. Every weekend in fall is filled with groans and cheers as high schools, colleges, and professional teams compete across the United States. Take a closer look at some memorable **pigskin** moments.

1993: The Comeback

The National Football League (NFL) playoff game in Buffalo, New York, on January 3, 1993, between the Buffalo Bills and the Houston Oilers was a game for the ages. In the first half, the Oilers quickly jumped to a 28–3 lead, eventually increasing the lead to as many as 32 points. A lot of **dejected** Bills fans left early, as they thought their beloved team had lost all hope of continuing in the playoffs. The Bills players, however, were **undeterred** and kept fighting—and scoring!

By the time the game was over, the Bills had won 41–38 in **overtime**. It was the biggest comeback in NFL history, and sports fans now refer to the game simply as "The Comeback."

Frank Reich sets up a pass in overtime.

The Reich Stuff

The Bills' quarterback during The Comeback was Frank Reich (RIKE). He knew about epic comebacks from his college days at the University of Maryland. Reich once helped his college team win after trailing by more than 28 points in a game!

David Tyree makes his now-famous helmet catch.

Pats on the Back

Tom Brady and the New England Patriots would pull off an upset of their own in Super Bowl LI in 2017. The Patriots came back from 25 points down in the second half to force the game into overtime for the first time in Super Bowl history. The Patriots ended up beating the Atlanta Falcons 34–28 in a truly wild game.

2007: The Helmet Catch

In 2007, the New England Patriots headed to Super Bowl XLII **undefeated**. They were only the second team in the history of the NFL to get that far without losing a single game. The Patriots would face the New York Giants for the final match of the **postseason**. The game was close, but Patriots quarterback Tom Brady threw a touchdown pass with less than three minutes remaining to give his team the lead.

The Giants got the ball next, and quarterback Eli Manning threw a long pass to receiver David Tyree. Giants' fans held their breath as Tyree pinned the ball on his helmet with his right hand! The play set up a touchdown that gave the Giants the 17–14 victory and the Patriots their first, and harshest, loss of the season.

THINK LINK

- How would you handle losing in the final seconds of a game?
- What would you say to your teammates after a heartbreaking loss?
- What lessons can you learn from a loss that you might not learn from a win?

1981: The Mistake by the Lake

The 1980 Cleveland Browns became known as the **Kardiac** Kids after 13 of their 16 regular-season games were decided in the final two minutes. The Kardiac Kids broke the hearts of many other teams' fans that year by winning 11 games to make it to the playoffs. The Browns' quarterback, Brian Sipe, was even named the league's Most Valuable Player (MVP).

The 1980 season was the first time that the Browns had qualified for the postseason since 1972. Expectations were high as they headed into the playoff game against the Oakland Raiders. Needing only two points to win, Sipe marched his team to the Raiders' 14-yard line with just 46 seconds left in the game. Instead of kicking a short field goal for the win, the team tried one last pass on a play called Red Right 88. Unfortunately for Browns' fans, Sipe's pass was **intercepted** in the end zone. Just like that, the Kardiac Kids' dramatic season was over.

Frozen Football

The decision to try one more pass play instead of kicking a short field goal seemed **controversial** to many Browns' fans. The truth, however, was that the temperature that January day next to Lake Erie was −5 degrees Fahrenheit (−20.5 degrees Celsius). The field was too icy to make a field goal a sure thing, solidifying the game as the "Mistake by the Lake."

Brian Sipe walks off the field after his season-ending interception.

Playing for a President

In 1984, fan-favorite Brian Sipe broke fans' hearts again. This time it was by leaving the Browns to play for the New Jersey Generals, a team in the newly formed United States Football League. At the time, future president Donald Trump owned the New Jersey Generals.

Morgan William shoots her game-winning basket over Gabby Williams.

Size Is a State of Mind

Bulldogs' guard Morgan William is nicknamed "Itty Bitty" because of her small **stature**. William is listed as only 5'5" (165 centimeters). That didn't stop her from making the big shot over the Huskies' 5'11" (180 cm) Gabby Williams.

The Way The Ball Bounces

In 1891, a teacher in Springfield, Massachusetts, named James Naismith nailed two peach baskets at each end of a gym. Naismith had teams try to throw a ball into each basket. From that day forward, the world of sports was forever changed by the invention of basketball.

2017: A Real Dog Fight!

In the 2017 women's college basketball tournament, the University of Connecticut Huskies faced the Mississippi State Bulldogs with the winner moving on to play in the national championship game. On paper, it didn't appear it would be much of a game. The Huskies were on an amazing 111-game winning **streak**, and they had won the previous four national championships.

The Bulldogs were tough, though, and the game went into overtime. The score was tied 64–64 when Bulldogs' guard Morgan William made the game-winning basket with no time remaining. The Huskies were absolutely **devastated**, as they had not lost a game in nearly three years.

Winning Streaks

Between 2001 and 2003, the Huskies' women's basketball team won 70 games in a row. Between 2008 and 2010, it won 90 games in a row. The 2014–2017 streak was 111 games. How far will its next streak go?

Butler's Ronald Nored dribbles past Duke's Kyrie Irving.

No Fluke

The Bulldogs returned to the men's tournament the following year, only to lose in the final game yet again. Despite the losses, Butler came to be seen as a major college basketball power.

2010: The Butler (Almost) Did It

Indiana is **synonymous** with basketball. Basketball greats John Wooden, Larry Bird, and Steve Alford were all born there. The movie *Hoosiers* (1986) was based on the true story of a small high school team that won the state championship in 1954. Indiana University has won five national titles.

In 2010, the little-known Butler Bulldogs added to the state's **lore**. Butler made it all the way to the final game of the men's college basketball tournament, where it faced three-time national champions, the Duke Blue Devils. The Bulldogs put up a fight that only ended as a final shot bounced off the rim as the buzzer sounded, making the final score 61–59. The following day, then-President Barack Obama called the team. He told them that even though they lost, they played a great game and showed tremendous heart.

A Hoosier Home

Butler plays its home games in Hinkle Fieldhouse. It is the sixth-oldest college basketball arena still in use in the United States. Milan High School won its miraculous state championship there in 1954, and the climactic game in *Hoosiers* was filmed on this beloved court.

2016: In the Final Seconds

The Golden State Warriors won an NBA-record 73 games in the 2015–2016 regular season. Stephen Curry was selected as the league's **unanimous** MVP. During the regular season, Curry had made a record 402 three-point shots.

As the Warriors headed into Game 5 of the best-of-seven NBA Finals, they were confident they could win. They were up three games to one and were ready to **clinch** their second straight title. LeBron James and the Cleveland Cavaliers, however, had other plans, winning Games 5 and 6 to tie the series at three games each.

The lead went back and forth in Game 7, before Curry missed a shot with just seconds left. The Warriors' Marreese Speights (muh-REESE SPAYTS) **rebounded** the ball and shot a three-pointer, but he also missed. The late misses sealed the Warriors' fate and gave the 93–89 win, and the championship, to the Cavaliers.

Return of the Warriors

Warriors' fans were crushed by the loss, but they would not have to wait long for their team's trophy. The Warriors and the Cavaliers met again in the 2017 finals. In that series, Golden State won four games and lost one to take the championship.

Golden State's Stephen Curry tries to block Cleveland's LeBron James during Game 7 of the 2016 NBA Finals.

Return of the King

LeBron James played for the Cavaliers from 2003 to 2010, before leaving to win two championships for the Miami Heat. Although he upset many Cavaliers fans, they welcomed him back to Cleveland in 2014. His one goal was to win a championship for the city. He did that just two years later.

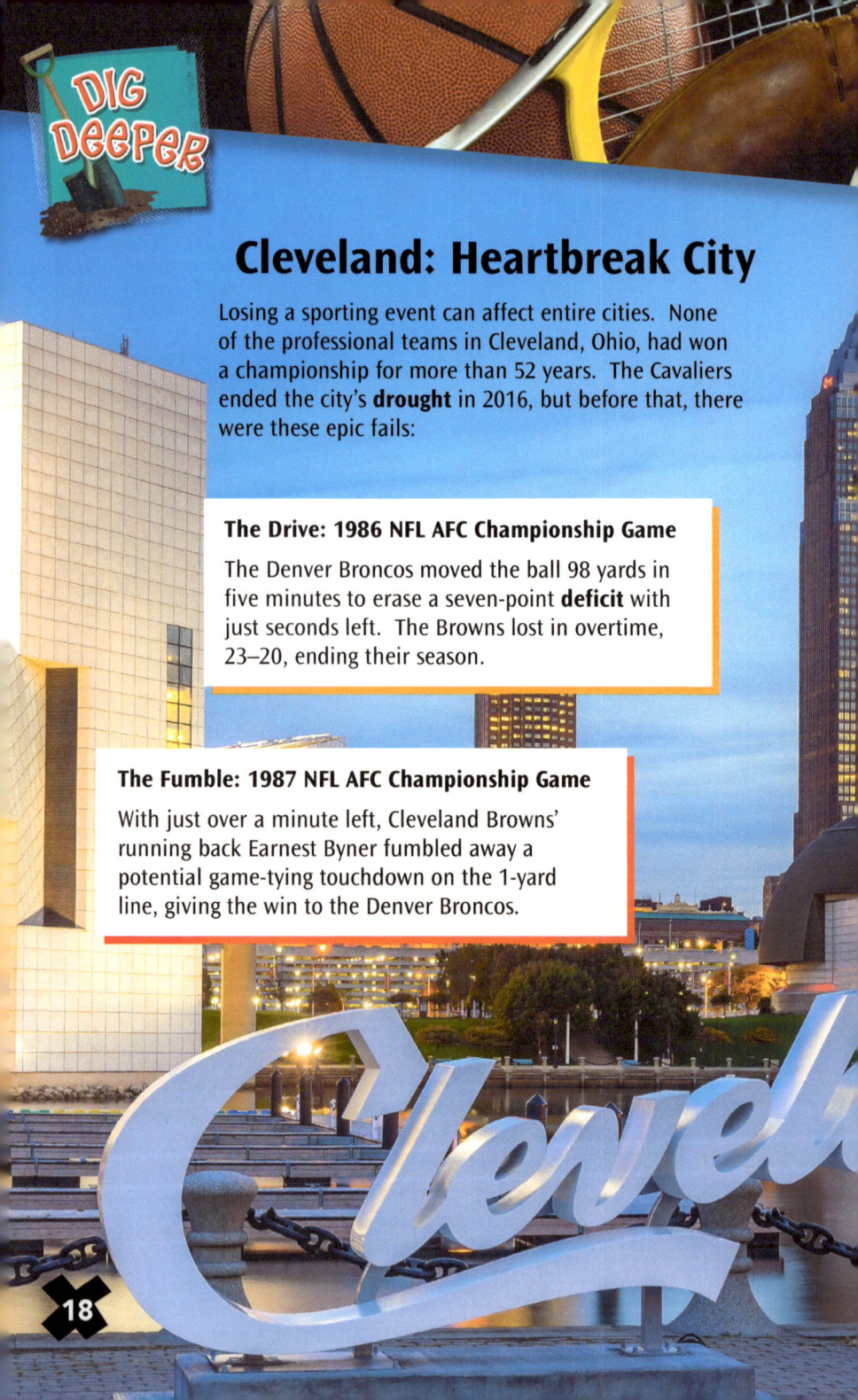

Dig Deeper

Cleveland: Heartbreak City

Losing a sporting event can affect entire cities. None of the professional teams in Cleveland, Ohio, had won a championship for more than 52 years. The Cavaliers ended the city's **drought** in 2016, but before that, there were these epic fails:

The Drive: 1986 NFL AFC Championship Game

The Denver Broncos moved the ball 98 yards in five minutes to erase a seven-point **deficit** with just seconds left. The Browns lost in overtime, 23–20, ending their season.

The Fumble: 1987 NFL AFC Championship Game

With just over a minute left, Cleveland Browns' running back Earnest Byner fumbled away a potential game-tying touchdown on the 1-yard line, giving the win to the Denver Broncos.

The Shot: 1989 NBA Playoffs

Chicago Bulls' Michael Jordan dashed the dreams of Cavaliers' fans with a last-second shot to win the game.

The Collapse: 1997 MLB World Series

The Cleveland Indians led by one run in the final inning of Game 7 but ended up losing in **extra innings** to the Florida Marlins.

The Meltdown: 2009 NBA Conference Finals

The Cavaliers had the NBA's best record and were undefeated in the playoffs before losing the series 4–2 to the Orlando Magic.

Take Your Base

Up until the 2003 baseball season, the Chicago Cubs and the Boston Red Sox were considered by many to be failures. At that time, Chicago hadn't won a title since 1908; Boston's last title was in 1918.

2003: Cubbies Come Close

In Game 6 of the 2003 playoffs, the Chicago Cubs were leading the Florida Marlins 3–0 in the top of the eighth inning. As outfielder Moisés Alou (moy-SEHS uh-LOO) attempted to catch a foul ball, a Cubs' fan in the stands named Steve Bartman tried to catch it, too, not realizing Alou could make the catch. Bartman accidentally **deflected** it away from Alou, and the ball fell to the ground. If Alou had caught the ball, it would have been the second out in the inning, and the Cubs would have been one step closer to their first World Series appearance since 1945. The play caused the Cubs to lose **momentum** and eventually the game and the series.

Curse of the Billy Goat

During the 1945 World Series, Cubs' fan William Sianis (see-EH-nihs) was not allowed to enter the Cubs' stadium because his pet goat, Murphy, smelled too bad. Sianis cursed the team, saying, "you are never going to win another World Series again." The curse was broken when the Cubs won the 2016 World Series.

Steve Bartman deflects the ball away from Cubs outfielder Moisés Alou.

Blaming Bartman

Just after the Bartman incident, Cubs' shortstop Alex Gonzalez committed an **error** that would have ended the inning. But the majority of Cubs' fans still blamed Bartman for the team's loss in the playoffs. Bartman went into hiding for years after the game because of the negative reactions he received from other fans.

Aaron Boone hits a walk-off home run in the 11th inning of the 2003 American League Championship Series.

Physical Challenge Accepted

Pitcher Jim Abbott was born without his right hand. That, however, didn't stop him from becoming an **elite** athlete, playing 10 seasons of professional baseball. He even pitched a no-hitter as a member of the New York Yankees in 1993. During that game, not a single member of the other team got a hit.

2003: Boone Beats Boston

In 2003, the Boston Red Sox were playing incredible baseball and looked certain to overcome their losing ways. However, to get to the World Series, they would have to defeat their biggest rival, the New York Yankees. After six games of a seven-game series, Boston and New York were tied with three wins apiece.

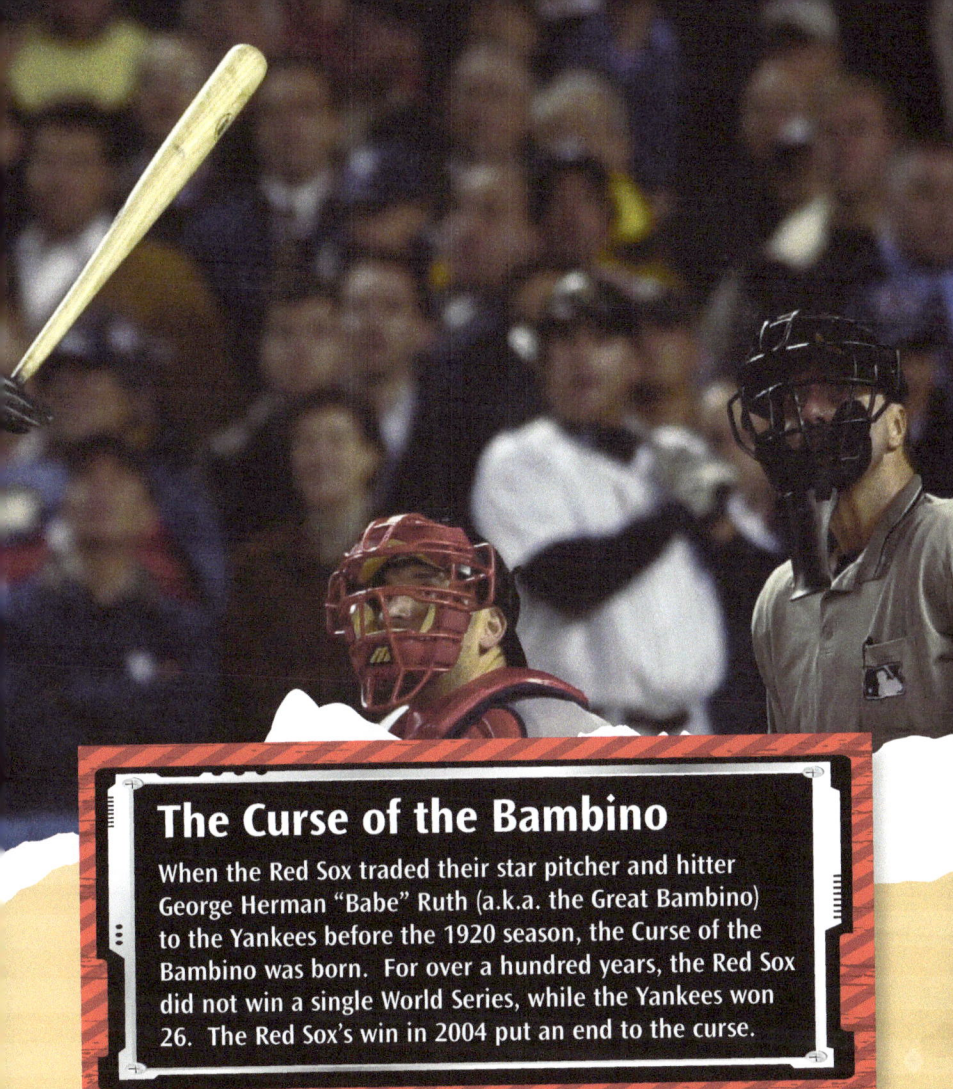

The Curse of the Bambino

When the Red Sox traded their star pitcher and hitter George Herman "Babe" Ruth (a.k.a. the Great Bambino) to the Yankees before the 1920 season, the Curse of the Bambino was born. For over a hundred years, the Red Sox did not win a single World Series, while the Yankees won 26. The Red Sox's win in 2004 put an end to the curse.

    The much-anticipated Game 7 began in New York's legendary Yankee Stadium. With a 5–2 lead, the Red Sox appeared to be on the brink of winning the game and going to the World Series; but the Yankees charged back, tying the score and sending the game into extra innings. A **walk-off home run** by Aaron Boone sent the Yankees to the World Series for the fifth time in six years, and sent Red Sox fans home, heartbroken at the loss.

Dig Deeper

Boston Red Sox, 86-Year Title Drought

1918: Red Sox win World Series over Chicago Cubs

1920: The Curse of the Bambino begins

1946 & 1967: Red Sox lose two World Series to St. Louis Cardinals in Game 7

1975: Red Sox lose World Series to Cincinnati Reds in Game 7

1986: Red Sox lose World Series to New York Mets in Game 7

2004: World Series Champions, over St. Louis Cardinals

Chicago Cubs, 108-Year Title Drought

1908: Chicago Cubs win World Series over Detroit Tigers

1910: Cubs lose World Series to Philadelphia Athletics

1918–1938: Cubs lose in five different World Series

1945: The Curse of the Billy Goat begins; Cubs lose World Series to Detroit Tigers

2003: Bartman incident occurs; Cubs fail to advance to the World Series

2016: World Series Champions, over Cleveland Indians

International Incidences

Sports are popular around the world, and two of the biggest sporting events are the Olympic Games and the World Cup. Each event attracts athletes and teams from many nations, including the United States.

2004: Running on Empty

Paula Radcliffe was the favorite to win a gold medal in the marathon at the 2004 Olympic Games in Athens, Greece. She was also Great Britain's best gold medal hope in any event. Radcliffe was in the leading group for the first 15 miles, but by mile 22, she had fallen to fourth place and was fading fast. The day of the marathon was very **humid**, with temperatures of about 95° F (35° C). Radcliffe slowed down and eventually stopped and sat down on the curb, unable to continue. Her self-removal from the race made headlines in Great Britain, with some reporters calling her a quitter. However, what the public didn't know at the time was that Radcliffe had suffered an injury to her leg two weeks prior and was running in horrible pain.

All Greek to Me

The first modern Olympic Games were held in 1896 in Athens, Greece. The first marathon race honored the Greek messenger who, in 490 B.C., ran for nearly 25 mi. (40 km) from the town of Marathon to Athens. His message was that the Greeks had been victorious over the Persians. After delivering his message, the messenger collapsed from exhaustion and died.

Paula Radcliffe sits on a curb at mile 22 of the marathon.

Back on Top

Less than three months after her failure at the 2004 Olympic Games, Radcliffe finished first in the New York City Marathon. "It's important to come back and run well," Radcliffe said about being on top again. "It's just important to be back feeling happy and feeling like myself again."

Jordyn Wieber and other members of the U.S. team practice before the 2012 Olympic Games.

The Fierce and Final Five

Jordyn Wieber, Gabby Douglas, McKayla Maroney, Aly Raisman, and Kyla Ross were all part of the Fierce Five. Four years later, in Rio de Janeiro, new team members Simone Biles, Laurie Hernandez, and Madison Kocian joined Douglas and Raisman. This new team, called The Final Five, conquered as well, again winning the team gold.

2012: From Failure to Fierceness

Gymnast Jordyn Wieber was at the top of her game going into the 2012 Olympic Games in London, England. She was the **reigning** U.S. national champion and world champion and was widely considered the best bet to win the gold medal. But it all came crashing down as she failed to qualify for the finals. Even on her own squad, she finished in third place. Wieber would have to watch her teammate Gabby Douglas take the gold medal.

Just two days after that heartbreaking disappointment, however, Wieber led the U.S. team in the team event, with the United States going on to win team gold for the first time since 1996. Instead of being remembered for what she didn't accomplish, she is remembered for being one of The Fierce Five—the nickname the team gave themselves.

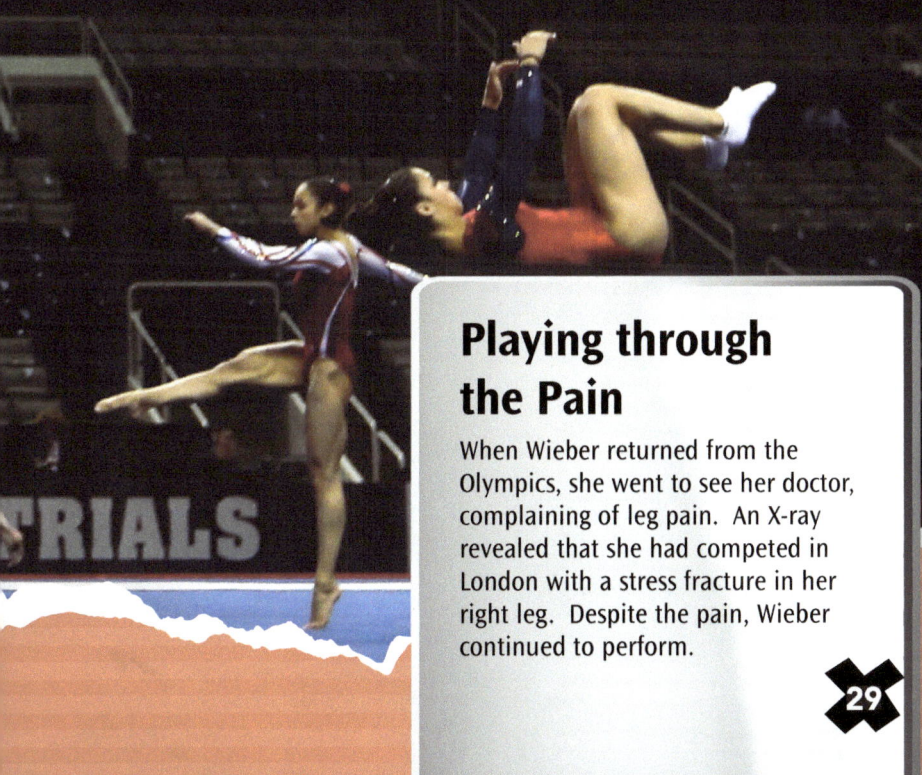

Playing through the Pain

When Wieber returned from the Olympics, she went to see her doctor, complaining of leg pain. An X-ray revealed that she had competed in London with a stress fracture in her right leg. Despite the pain, Wieber continued to perform.

Another Upset

Brazil wasn't the only team to have a shocking loss in the 2014 World Cup. The Spanish National Team went into the tournament as the winners of both the 2010 World Cup and the 2012 Euros. They were the favorite to win the whole tournament. But after losing their first two of three games, Spain was eliminated before making it out of the first stage of the tournament.

Brazilian midfielder Oscar lies on the field after his team's semifinal loss to Germany.

2014: A World Cup Catastrophe

The greatest success any nation's soccer team can achieve is to be crowned the champion of the World Cup. The tournament is held every four years, and nations from across the globe compete just to be invited. Only 32 teams make the final cut. In 2014, the World Cup was held in Brazil, a proud soccer country that had won five titles previously.

The Brazilians were undefeated in the tournament when they played their first **semifinal**. Their match against Germany ended in a stunning loss. Germany won the match 7–1, the largest margin of victory in a World Cup semifinal in the history of the tournament. Germany would go on to defeat Argentina in the final game, winning the country's fourth World Cup.

The End of a Streak

Before Brazil's loss, they had a 62-match unbeaten streak at home in competitive play. The winning streak started in 1975. After the loss, local reporters called the 2014 World Cup loss a national humiliation.

One-on-One Losses

When a team loses, players can rely on their teammates to comfort them. However, in many sports, such as tennis and golf, players face off in one-on-one competitions. It can be much more difficult to overcome epic defeat if someone has to do it alone.

1984: McEnroe's Meltdown

At the French Open in 1984, John McEnroe was in the middle of one of the best tennis seasons ever. He went into the final round with a 42-match winning streak, a record at the time. Then, during the final, a courtside cameraman's headset started making noise, which upset the hot-tempered American. McEnroe lost his **composure** and screamed at the cameraman, the umpire, and anyone else who would listen.

John McEnroe hits the ball back to Ivan Lendl during the 1984 French Open.

The crowd turned against McEnroe, who would eventually lose the tournament to Ivan Lendl, thereby breaking his amazing winning streak. In his autobiography, *You Cannot Be Serious* (2002), McEnroe wrote that it was the worst loss of his life. He wrote that it was "a devastating defeat. Sometimes, it still keeps me up nights."

Lendl's Loss

Five years later, in 1989, Lendl had his own stunning collapse at the French Open. His opponent, a 17-year-old American named Michael Chang, was having bad legs cramps, and it looked like it would be an easy victory for Lendl. However, Chang fought through his pain to win the match and eventually won the tournament.

1996: No More Norman

Golf tournaments are usually played over four days, from Thursday to Sunday. So, when Australian Greg Norman opened the first day of the 1996 Masters tournament in Augusta, Georgia, by tying the course record and continued to hold the lead through three days of play, Norman was sure of a win as the final round began on Sunday.

Norman was one of the most popular golfers on tour with a sizable following of fans. He also had an impressive record. Norman went into the 1996 Masters having won two British Opens; tied for second-place in two previous Masters; and placed second in two U.S. Opens and two Professional Golf Association (PGA) Championships.

However, the pressure got to Norman, and he lost his cool—and the tournament—in epic fashion. He missed enough shots on the fourth day to erase all of his hard work from the first three days. After that stunning collapse, Norman never won the Masters again.

Moon Landing

Alan Shepherd was an avid golfer, but he never played professionally. However, he holds the record for playing on the most far-out course ever. As a NASA astronaut, Shepherd brought a golf club onboard the *Apollo 14* spacecraft and actually hit two golf balls on the surface of the moon!

Greg Norman attempts to hit his golf ball out of a sand trap at the 1996 Masters tournament.

Shark Attack

Norman has blond hair, was an aggressive golfer, and was born and raised in Australia. People soon began calling Norman "The Great White Shark." Even though some people thought Norman couldn't handle pressure because of his 1996 Masters collapse, Norman was elected into the World Golf Hall of Fame in 2001.

Greatest Golfer of All Time?

Professional golf has four huge tournaments each year, and they are collectively called the "Majors." The tournaments are: the Masters, the PGA Championship, the U.S. Open, and the British Open. Although many have failed to win these key tournaments, no one has had more heartbreaks than Jack Nicklaus. He has finished second-place in 19 Majors and third-place in 9 others.

Nicklaus, however, isn't a loser by any means. In fact, to many, he's the greatest golfer ever, as he also holds the record for the most Majors' victories—18. It just proves that even the best can lose time and again and still come out a champion.

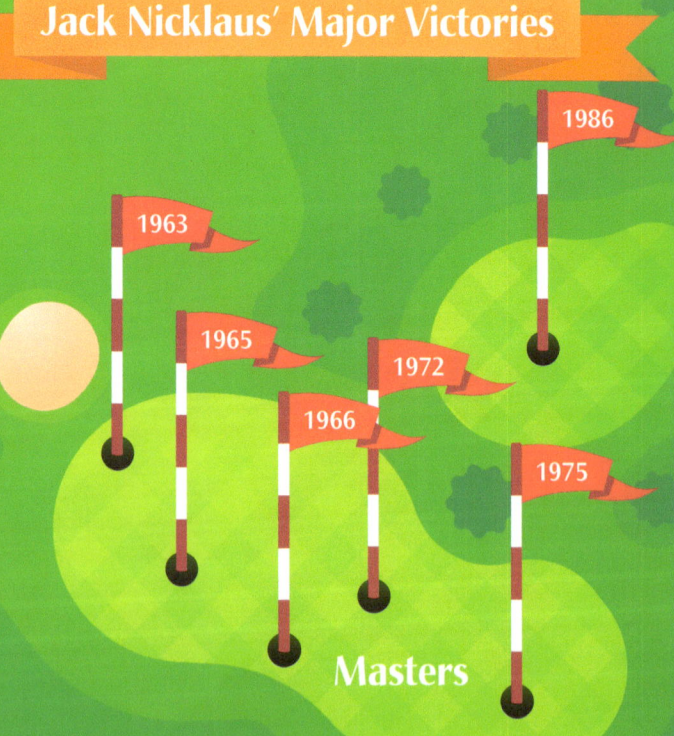

Jack Nicklaus' Major Victories

1963, 1965, 1966, 1972, 1975, 1986 — Masters

Like Mother, Like Daughter

Rousey won the bronze medal in judo, a style of martial arts, at the 2008 Olympic Games in Beijing, China. This was a memorable moment for Rousey. Just 24 years before she won her Olympic medal, Rousey's mother became the first U.S. woman to win a world judo title.

Mixing It Up

UFC is a mixed martial arts (MMA) promotional company that started in 1993. MMA is a contact sport that allows fighters to punch, kick, and wrestle their opponents. It is similar to boxing but with kicking and other fighting techniques allowed.

2015: A Knockout Sport

The Ultimate Fighting Championship (UFC) has only been around for a few years, but it's quickly become one of the hottest sports around. In 2015, no UFC athlete was more popular than Ronda "Rowdy" Rousey. She had appeared on several magazine covers and had starred in movies and commercials.

Rousey's seventh title defense on November 14, 2015, put her up against little-known **underdog** Holly Holm. Early in the second round, Holm punched Rousey in the face and then kicked her in the neck, which quickly knocked out Rousey. It was Rousey's first loss, and her nearly three-year reign as champion was over. She came back a year later in an attempt to recapture her title but lost again. After that, Rousey shocked the UFC community when she announced she was retiring from the sport she had helped make popular.

Holly Holm knocks down Ronda Rousey in the 2015 UFC Championship.

Making an Effort

Athletes win and lose every day—they face triumph and heartbreak, glory and disappointment. They put a lot of time and effort into practicing, playing, and watching sports, so when they lose, it is common to see them hang their heads and look devastated. However, losing should not always be seen as a bad thing.

Legendary football coach Vincent Lombardi of the Green Bay Packers is often misquoted as saying, "Winning isn't everything, it's the only thing." Lombardi's actual words, however, leave a far deeper and more inspiring message— "Winning is not everything, but making the effort to win is."

These words are a powerful message to live by. At the end of the day, it does not matter whether you win or lose as long as you do your best. It is the effort, not the result, which truly matters.

Be a Good Sport

"For most of my life, I have believed that success is found in the running of the race," wrote legendary basketball coach John Wooden. "How you run the race—your planning, preparation, practice, and performance—counts for everything. Winning or losing is a by-product, an aftereffect, of that effort."

STOP! THINK...

Ty Cobb is considered by many people to be the greatest hitter of all time. He had a lifetime batting average of .366, which is still the highest lifetime batting average in Major League Baseball history.

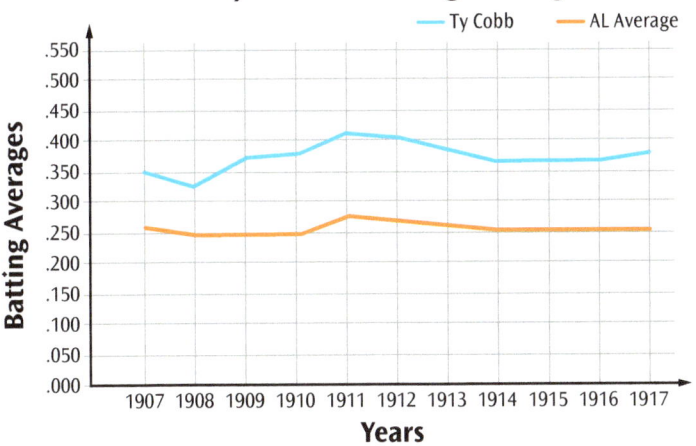

- What do you notice about Cobb's batting averages from 1907 to 1917 compared to the American League (AL) average during the same time?

- Cobb only made it to the base safely about 36 times out of every 100. Why might he still be considered the greatest hitter of all time even though he failed to get on base over 60 percent of the time?

- What do you notice about Cobb's batting average in 1907 (when he was 20 years old) versus 1917 (when he was 30 years old)? Does that trend surprise you? Why or why not?

Glossary

agony—extreme physical or mental pain

clinch—to ensure the winning of something

composure—calmness of mind, appearance, or manner

controversial—relating to or causing much disagreement or discussion

deficit—the amount by which a team or person is behind in a game or contest

deflected—caused a moving object to change direction

dejected—sad because of a loss or failure

devastated—in extreme emotional pain or sadness

drought—a long period of time in which something that is expected or desired does not happen

elite—successful or powerful in a group

error—a mistake

extra innings—the extension of a baseball or softball game, beyond the usual nine innings, to break a tie

humid—having a lot of moisture in the air so that it feels damp

intercepted—caught by an opponent

kardiac—play on the word *cardiac*, which is something relating to the heart

lore—the traditional beliefs, stories, and knowledge that relate to a certain subject, place, or group of people

momentum—the force that allows something to continue moving or growing in strength

overtime—extra time added to the end of a game in some sports to break a tie

pigskin—nickname for the sport of football, referring to the old footballs that used to be made with leather from the skin of pigs

postseason—a period of time after the regular season of a sport in which teams play against each other to determine the champion

rebounded—caught a basketball after a shot has missed the basket

reigning—used to describe the best, most important, or most powerful person during a specific time

semifinal—match or game that decides which people or teams will be in the final part of a competition

showcased—showed the abilities of someone or something in a positive way

stature—a person's height

streak—a period of continual wins or losses

synonymous—strongly suggesting that a certain idea or quality is closely connected with something else

unanimous—agreed on by everyone

undefeated—not having any losses or defeats for a period of time

underdog—a person or team that is expected to lose a game or contest

undeterred—not discouraged or stopped by criticism or problems

walk-off home run—a game-ending hit that allows a home team batter to go around the bases and score a run

Index

Abbott, Jim, 22
Alou, Moisés, 20–21
Apollo 14, 34
Bartman, Steve, 20–21, 25
Boston Red Sox, 20, 22–24
Brady, Tom, 8–9
Brazil, 30–31
British Open, 34, 36–37
Buffalo Bills, 6–7
Butler Bulldogs, 14–15
Byner, Earnest, 18
Chang, Michael, 33
Chicago Cubs, 20–21, 24–25
Cleveland Browns, 10–11, 18
Cleveland Cavaliers, 16–19
Cleveland Indians, 19, 25
Cobb, Ty, 41
Curry, Stephen, 16–17
Curse of the Bambino, 23–24
Curse of the Billy Goat, 20, 25
Douglas, Gabby, 28–29
Duke Blue Devils, 14–15
Fierce Five, 28–29
Final Five, 28
French Open, 32–33
Germany, 30–31
Golden State Warriors, 16–17
Greece, 26
Hinkle Fieldhouse, 15
Holm, Holly, 39
Hoosiers, 15
Houston Oilers, 6
Irving, Kyrie, 14
James, LeBron, 16–17
Kardiac Kids, 10
Lendl, Ivan, 33
Lombardi, Vincent, 40
Majors, 36
Manning, Eli, 9
Masters, 34–36
McEnroe, John, 32–33
Milan High School, 15
Mississippi State Bulldogs, 12–13
Naismith, James, 13
NASA, 34
New England Patriots, 8–9

New Jersey Generals, 11
New York City Marathon, 27
New York Giants, 9
New York Yankees, 22–23
Nicklaus, Jack, 36
Nored, Ronald, 14
Norman, Greg, 34–35
Oakland Raiders, 10
Obama, Barack, 15
Olympic Games, 4, 26–29, 38
Oscar, 30
Professional Golf Association (PGA) Championship, 34, 36–37
Radcliffe, Paula, 26–27
Red Right 88, 10
Reich, Frank, 7
Rousey, Ronda "Rowdy", 38–39
Ruth, George Herman "Babe", 23
Shepherd, Alan, 34
Sianis, William, 20
Sipe, Brian, 10–11

Spain, 30
Speights, Marreese, 16
Super Bowl LI, 8
Super Bowl XLII, 9
Trump, Donald, 11
Tyree, David, 8–9
Ultimate Fighting Championship (UFC), 38–39
United States Football League, 11
University of Connecticut Huskies, 12–13
U.S. Open, 34, 36–37
Wide World of Sports, 4
Wieber, Jordyn, 28–29
William, Morgan, 12–13
Williams, Gabby, 12
World Cup, 26, 30–31

Check It Out!

Books

National Geographic Kids. 2016. *Weird but True Sports: 300 Wacky Facts About Awesome Athletics*. Washington, D.C.: National Geographic Children's Books.

Alexander, Kwame. 2014. *The Crossover*. New York: HMH Books for Young Readers.

Herzog, Brad. 2014. *Inspiring Stories of Sportsmanship (Count on Me: Sports)*. Minneapolis: Free Spirit Publishing.

Videos

NFL Films. 2013. *NFL Greatest Games: The Comeback*. NFL Productions.

ESPN Films. 2009–. *30 for 30*. ESPN Films.

Websites

ESPN. *Hall of Flameout: The 25 worst collapses in sports history*. www.espn.com/espn/story/_/id/16685483.

Sports Illustrated. *100 Greatest Moments in Sports History*. www.si.com/100-greatest/.

Try It!

Imagine you are a radio announcer for one of the events mentioned in the book. It is your job to describe what is happening with enough enthusiasm that listeners feel as though they are watching the event unfold, too.

- ✖ Choose an event from the book.

- ✖ Record yourself as you describe when and where the event is taking place.

- ✖ Explain to listeners what is happening.

- ✖ Be sure to remain enthusiastic during your reporting.

- ✖ Share the recording with your family or a classmate.

- ✖ Was your play-by-play description unexpected, sad, funny, or otherwise memorable? How?

About the Author

When Roger Sipe was flipping through the TV channels as a young boy in 1980, he happened upon the Kardiac Kids and Brian Sipe (no relation). From that day forward, he was a life-long Cleveland Browns fan. Although his Browns never reached the Super Bowl while he was growing up, he learned from them how to handle defeat with grace and just enjoy competing. His football career ended in high school, when he realized he was a better writer than an athlete. Today, he lives in Indianapolis, Indiana, with his wife, Nicole, and two sons, who he hopes will grow up to be good sports.

www.ingramcontent.com/pod-product-compliance
Lightning Source LLC
Chambersburg PA
CBHW041505010526
44118CB00001B/24